Walking in the
Northern Dales

Wensleydale - Swaledale - Teesdale

Compiled by
The Ramblers' Association
(North Yorkshire and South Durham Area)

D1328793

DALESMAN BOOKS

1973

35p.

THE DALESMAN PUBLISHING COMPANY LTD.,
CLAPHAM (via Lancaster), YORKSHIRE

First Published 1973

© Ramblers' Association (North Yorkshire and
South Durham Area) 1973.

ISBN : O 85206 208 7

Printed in Great Britain by
GEO. TODD & SON,
Marlborough Street, Whitehaven.

CONTENTS

The front cover sketch of a farm near Whaw in Arkengarthdale is by Frank Armstrong, and the back cover of
Romaldkirk in Teesdale by Alec Wright. The maps are
by R. Gibbs.

Near the Pennine Way, Keld (drawn by S. Warburton).

PREFACE

AS EACH YEAR goes by, more and more people of all ages are taking to the hills for recreation. With the car carefully parked, a circular walk of ten miles or so fills a day with joyful and enlightening experience. Fellside and dale in North Yorkshire and South Durham offer fantastic variety and an unrivalled opportunity to find a tranquil solitude which all of us need from time to time.

Many of the walks detailed in this book are wholly or partially within the boundaries of the Yorkshire Dales National Park; those outside the Park are no less pleasant, for the boundary line drawn round the Dales rested more often on political divisions than on considerations of landscape quality.

The setting up of a National Park does not, of itself, confer upon the public any additional rights of access to any part of the countryside. With this point in mind the authors have carefully chosen routes along Public Rights of Way; if these are followed there is no possibility of the law regarding trespass being invoked.

One final point — the people at the Dalesman Publishing Company are very good friends of mine and at my request have printed the Country Code somewhere among the pages of this book. Please, seek it out and follow it : the ten precepts are the key to good relations between the townsman who uses the countryside for recreation, and the countryman who uses it as a workshop. We are all interdependent.

WILF PROCTOR,

Information Officer,
Yorkshire Dales National Park.

FOREWORD

THIS BOOK of rambles has been prepared by members of the North Yorkshire and South Durham Area of the Ramblers' Association in collaboration with the Darlington Rucksack Club and the Darlington and Hartlepool C.H.A./H.F. Rambling Clubs. All walks are circular and suitable for the motorist. Details of public transport facilities are shown where applicable. The leading public transport operator in the area is the United Automobile Services of Grange Road, Darlington, whose public time-table gives details of all the relevant bus times.

The routes vary in length from five to ten miles, and are suitable for all who enjoy a pleasant country walk. Whatever walk the reader follows, he should be sure he is adequately shod and is carrying some form of waterproof clothing. Many of the walks cross rough moorland and it is easy to sprain an ankle while walking in such an area if one's shoes are too lightweight. High heels are most unsuitable. It may be fine weather when you start your walk, but this does not necessarily mean it will be fine when you finish, hence the need for a waterproof. Those readers wishing to do those walks which ascend to over 1,500 feet should have some recent experience of walking distances, and should also take particular cognisance of the routine safety precautions.

In preparing these walks, care has been taken to keep to established rights of way, a practice which has been departed from in certain forest areas where members of the public are permitted to follow the forest rides even though they do not appear on the definitive map. When walking in forestry, be particularly careful in dry weather not to start a fire. Please remember, when crossing farmland, that this is the source of someone's livelihood, and take particular care not to trample on crops and not to leave gates open whereby cattle can stray from one field to another. Further, if you have a dog, please keep it under control.

Lastly in this foreword, an explanatory note about the maps — where the dotted route is between two continuous lines, then the walk is at this point along a metalled road.

THE COUNTRY CODE

Guard against All Risk of Fire

Fasten All Gates

Keep Dogs under Proper Control

Keep to the Paths across Farm Land

Avoid Damaging Fences, Hedges and Walls

Leave No Litter

Safeguard Water Supplies

Protect Wild Life, Wild Plants and Trees

Go Carefully on Country Roads

Respect the Life of the Countryside

Cover Bridge, near Middleham (drawn by Alec Wright).

Wensleydale

COLSTERDALE

Starting Point : The village of East Witton, G.R. 145860.

Public Transport : East Witton is served by United Automobile Services Route 127 *(Hawes-Ripon).*

LEAVE East Witton along the minor road going in a southerly direction from the south-eastern corner of the village green, adjacent to the right-angle bend in the A6108 and to the bus stop. In a little over a hundred yards take the right fork to ascend the flanks of Witton Fell along Sowden Beck Road. The lane is sunken at first, but after passing through a gate becomes an enclosed track with forest on the right and an extensive view across the Vale of York on the left. In about a mile the route turns an acute right-hand bend, and in a short distance there is a gate ahead beyond which the track is no longer enclosed. Immediately before reaching this gate, pass through another gate on the left, and after crossing a field with a wall on the right, cross a beck to reach Sowden Beck House.

Keep the farm house on your right, pass through a couple of tubular steel gates and begin to ascend, still with the wall on your right, to the top of the moor. Pass through a gate, and keep straight ahead along a rough track through the heather. The route is boggy in parts, but the way is quite distinct. Soon the hills around Colsterdale and beyond to Masham Moor come into view, and you begin the descent into Colsterdale. Ultimately, after passing through a gate, the metalled road from Colsterdale House to Masham is reached. Follow this road down to the telephone box about half-a-mile further on, in the middle of a small hamlet, which is the greatest centre of population in this remote area.

To commence the walk back to East Witton, follow the road on the left just beyond the telephone box, signposted to Low Agra. Shortly before reaching this farm you pass through a gate, beyond which you should turn right up the hillside, keeping the forest-boundary wall immediately on your right. Keep climbing, cross a forestry track and pass through a field-gate to enter the pasture around Agra Farm itself. Make for the corner of the field immediately to the left of the farm-building, and pass through a small gate on the left to enter the forest. Follow the defined path through the forest, cross a wire fence at the opposite end by means of a wooden step stile, and then pass through the field-gate immediately opposite. Turn right to pass through another field-gate, and then keep straight on across the next field, making for the gate in the wall ahead just below the skyline.

Cross the beck by the footbridge, and ascend to pass through the gate you have seen ahead for some little time, to reach the track from Bales House to Tranmire just beyond the brow of the hill. Turn left here for a very short distance, and just before passing through a gate turn right with the stone wall on your left. This wall is a parish boundary, and every so often old boundary stones may be seen in its structure, presumably marking the western extremity of Mashamshire. Immediately before reaching the plantation, turn left to pass through a gate and then continue with the wall on your right. Descend and veer gradually to the left, passing through a gate into a field, to reach the metalled road at a road-junction at the western end of Ellingstring village.

Turn left along the metalled road, and follow it for three-quarters of a mile, round a right-angled right-hand bend,

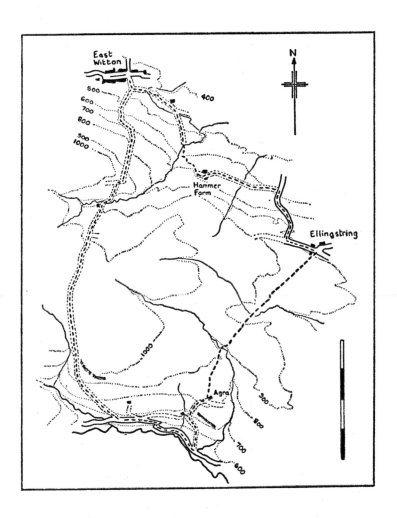

until a distinct farm track is reached on the left. Follow this track across the fields, through the buildings of Hammer Farm, to bear right beyond and descend to cross Deep Gill Beck on an enclosed track between stretches of woodland. Beyond this point the route is quite distinct back to East Witton. It keeps the farmbuildings of Waterloo Farm over on the right, and enters the village by the left fork at the bottom of Sowden Beck Road.   *Distance*: **9** *miles.*

LOWER WENSLEYDALE

Starting Point: *Centre of the village of Spennithorne,* G.R. 137890.

Public Transport: *The village is served by United Automobile Services Route 72. (Darlington - Northallerton - Bedale-Leyburn).*

STARTING FROM the church, go down the road away from the village and, after the second bend in the road, walk a few yards to cross a stile in the stone wall on the right. Turn to the left and walk round two sides of this field to a gap in the hedge in the corner. Go through the gap and keep to the hedge on the left, then through the first field-gate turn right and keep to the hedge on the right to the river bank.

Now keep to the river bank to Ulshaw Bridge. Do not cross the bridge but cross the road and enter a lane signposted to Danby Hall. At the first bend in this lane keep straight on, following the course of the river Ure, and soon you will enter the park in which stands Danby Hall, the seat of Mr. Simon Scrope, a representative of the family who have held Danby Estate for over 500 years. Much of the house is Elizabethan. On entering the park keep along the carriage drive until it turns towards the Hall. At this bend the right of way is straight ahead to a field-gate. Go through this gate and keep to the hedge on the right for

12

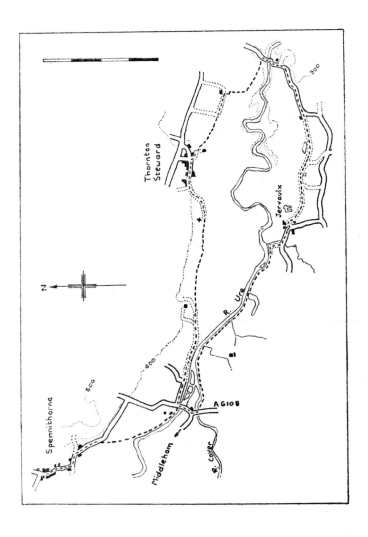

several fields until St. Oswald's church is reached, just before Thornton Steward. The original village of Thornton Steward once surrounded this church, but it has been long since deserted and the current village lies some little distance to the east.

Continue along the lane into the present-day village of Thornton Steward on its hillside above the river Ure, and on reaching the school turn off to the right and follow a short enclosed lane to the left. On reaching the fields cross two stiles and keep the same direction to a field-gate in the far corner, then keep to the hedge on the right until Woodhouse Farm is reached. Immediately before the farm, turn right through a field-gate, go over a stile by another field-gate, cross a narrow field and then keep close to the hedge on the left until a bridle gate is reached just before the river. Go through this gate and keep along the high embankment to Kilgram Bridge.

Cross the bridge and keep along the metalled road to reach the East Lodge of Jervaulx Park in half a mile. Follow the carriage drive, which is a right-of-way through the park, to reach the exit on to the Masham - Leyburn road near to Jervaulx Hall. The picturesque ruins of Jervaulx Abbey, and the Victorian Jervaulx Hall elegantly built in the Elizabethan style, are passed on the right. On reaching the main road turn right, and follow the highway for 300 yards until, immediately after crossing Harker Beck Bridge, a broad track is seen on the right parallel to the river Ure. Follow this track, which soon becomes a long and pleasant riverside walk, for one and a half miles to Cover Bridge, near the confluence of the rivers Ure and Cover. You will cross this bridge and within a few yards return to Ulshaw Bridge from where you can return to Spennithorne by the same route as the beginning of the walk.

The return route is to cross Ulshaw Bridge, turn left by Ulshaw Cottage and keep along the river bank for two fields. As the river bends sharply to the left, the footpath keeps the same direction close to the hedge on the left. Go through the field-gate in the corner, turn right and walk by the

14

hedge on the right. After passing through the gap in the corner, go to the right and keep round two sides of this field to the stone stile used at the beginning of the walk. Spennithorne is half a mile up the road.

Distance : 9¼ *miles.*

PEN HILL

Starting Point : *Centre of the village of Carlton-in-Coverdale, G.R. 064846.*

FROM THE CENTRE of the village walk to the east end and fork right along a lane signed "Unsuitable for Motorists". As the road turns left our route is forward on to an enclosed green lane, at the end of which you should continue to walk along the cart-road towards Howden Lodge, a stone building seen in the distance. Keep this building on the left and continue in a westerly direction, still along the cart-road, first by a wall on the left and then across open moor. The track passes through a gateway with no gate, then bears slightly to the right to go through the gap in the next wall. The track is now less distinct but still easy to follow as Waldendale and Bishopdale come into view with West Burton and Thoralby in the valley below. The track now keeps to the wall on the right and soon becomes a winding route descending into the valley of the Walden Beck.

At the junction of the stony lane and the valley road, there are remains of an old smelting mill complete with chimney and flue, reminders of the lead-mining industry which prospered in the dales one hundred years ago. Turn right along the metalled road and just before reaching Cote Bridge, by which the road crosses Walden Beck, pass through a field-gate on the right. Immediately divert away from the beck to go through a gate near an old building, then turn sharp left to cross a stile and walk towards a

15

footbridge over the beck. Do not cross the bridge, but make for a stile in the corner away from the beck. After crossing this stile the path goes to the left through a gate and passes the Riddings Farm buildings seen on the left.

Continue through a gap and a succession of stiles until an open field is reached. A turn to the left at this point leads into the village of West Burton, but your route is to a stile seen entering a small plantation. Cross the stile, and follow the path along the foot of the plantation. Soon after leaving the wood, the footpath inclines to the right to cross a stile at the top of the hill. It then goes to the left by the stone building and forward to pass through a gate on to a narrow lane known as Morpeth Gate, along which you go to the right. This is a green lane, three miles long, from which there is an ever-changing view stretching from the Cleveland Hills in the east to Bishopdale in the west.

Eventually the steep road coming up from West Witton is reached and your route continues to climb this road, turning right at Steeps Head Farm on the corner. The road continues to climb, then crosses a cattle-grid on to the open moor from where you may look across into Coverdale. The last mile-and-a-half is along this moor road, gradually descending into Coverdale and passing through Melmerby on the way. In Melmerby turn right for Carlton.

Distance : 10 *miles.*

THORALBY CIRCULAR

Starting Point : *Outside the George Inn in the centre of Thoralby village, G.R.* 002867.

TAKE THE LANE out of Thoralby village which passes the George Inn, and goes out in a westerly direction. Just before reaching the end of the village, turn right in to Haw Lane. Follow the lane round a series of right-hand and left-hand bends and, at the end of the lane, keep by the

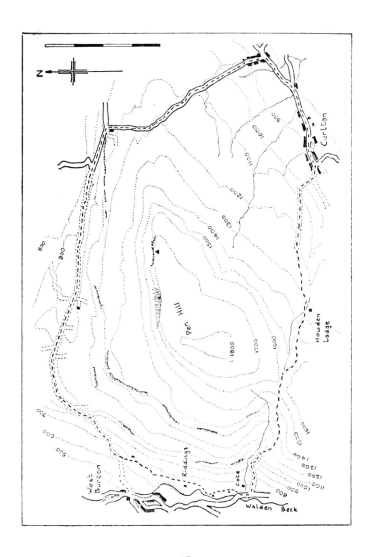

Z

Carlton

900
1000
1100
1200
1300
1400
1500

Pen Hill

1800
1700
1600

Howden
Lodge

1500
1400
1300
1200
1100
1000
900
800

800
900

700
600
500

West Burton

Riddings

Cote

Walden Beck

17

wall on the left with Gayle Ing Farm to the right. The cart road continues on in a westerly direction, sunken for a short distance, and then crosses two streams to the right. For a short stretch it is an enclosed track before becoming a broad green track ascending the hillside, with Kidstones Fell and Kidstones Scar away to the left.

As the moor levels out, keep to the wall on the left and pass through a field-gate. Then follow the line of the broken wall and wire fence on the right, at the end of which pass through another field-gate and make for a green hummock on the skyline. Walk straight forward on to an enclosed green lane, known as Carpley Green Road. Turn right and follow this for a little less than two miles, leaving the lane approximately one hundred yards beyond the first building on the right, after which directions must be followed closely.

Keep to the wall on the right and go through the next field-gate. Now walk half left uphill, keeping round the southern shoulder of Addlebrough, to a field-gate. Go through this gate and walk ahead to the next gate seen in the distance, keeping parallel to the wall on the right. Follow this wall, go through a bridle-gate and turn left, gradually veering away from the wall along a defined path to another gateway. Now follow a good track in a north-easterly direction, ensuring the easily-definable square keep of Bolton Castle on the opposite side of the dale is directly in front of you. Cross the next wide open pasture to the top right hand corner, then keep along the enclosed lane into Thornton Rust, a fine old Dales village.

To return to Thoralby retrace your steps along the enclosed lane which you have just traversed, and go through the first field-gate on the left after crossing the water-splash. Cross the first two fields by stiles, and keep the same direction to the top corner of the next field where you cross the left of two stiles. Still keeping the same direction, cross a railed gap and turn left. Cross a railed stile in the wall and continue, with a clump of trees away to the left. Drop down to cross Gill Beck and then go through a gap in the wall to reach Flout Moor Lane. Go left for 100 yards and

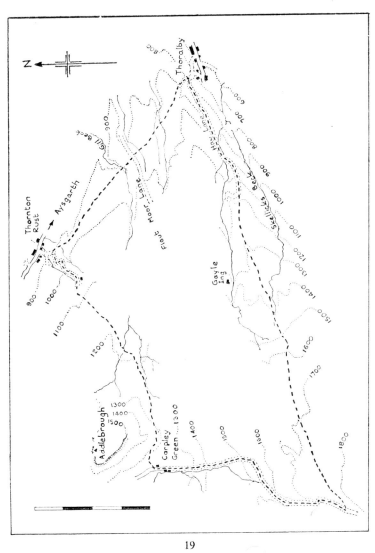

N

Thoralby

Thornton
Rust

Aysgarth

Gill Beck

800

900

600

700

High Lane

800

900

1000

Skell Gill Beck

1100

1200

1300

1400

1500

1600

1700

1800

Gayle
Ing

Flout Moor Lane

900

1000

1100

1200

1300
1400
1500

Addlebrough

Carpley
Green

1300

1400

1500

1600

then through a field-gate on the right. Look for a stile on the left, cross it and walk towards a few trees seen on the skyline. Now cross How Beck just beyond the T-junction of two walls and walk up to the few trees. Cross a stile to the right of the trees, then veer to the wall on the right and go through the gate. Finally keep to the wall on the left to Haw Lane and back to Thoralby.

Distance : 10½ *miles.*

ADDLEBROUGH

Starting Point : Centre of the village of Thornton Rust, G.R. 972889.

Public Transport : United Automobile Services Route 26 (Darlington - Hawes) passes through the village.

THE WALK commences opposite the village Institute where a narrow lane winds its way towards the moorland. A small stream has to be forded approximately 100 yards from the starting point, and your way is then half-left up a stony lane which is walled on both sides. After a few minor twists and bends, a sharp left-hand bend reveals approximately 100 yards of uphill until the walled lane doubles back on itself at a sharp right-hand bend. Further on a barn is passed on the left, and then the lane passes through a tubular steel gate and fords the West Beck.

Continue for a further 100 yards until the left-hand wall forms a field boundary and you approach open grassland. Turning half-left you will observe a stone wall on higher ground ahead of you and a grass track leading towards a field-gate in this wall. Passing through this gate, and keeping in the same direction, a steady climb of approximately a quarter of a mile will reveal a shallow dip ahead in which a small stream and some marshy ground lie. The track is indistinct in places, but careful observation will show it leading to two field-gates ahead in a stone wall. Make your way to the right-hand gate by crossing this marshy ground.

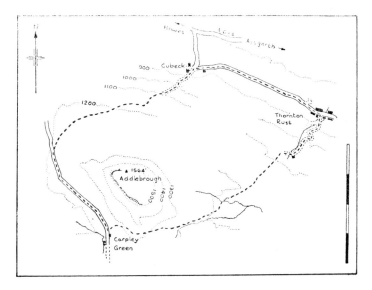

Pass through the gate and turn right, and continue in that direction with the stone wall on your right and a small stream on your left. After approximately a quarter of a mile, pass through a further gate in this wall on your right, and continue in the same general direction keeping the wall on your left.

You will soon observe two stone walls ahead with field-gates through which the track passes. Passing through the second of these gates and proceeding for another 20 yards, you will reach the highest point of the walk (1,340 ft.) on the southern slope of Addlebrough. Looking back, Pen Hill is clearly visible, together with the main valley of Wensleydale. To the left are fine moorland views, while ahead the farmstead of Carpley Green is not too distant. To gain the road at this latter point, gently descend with the wall on your left towards a field-gate, and after passing through turn left and follow the stone wall towards the road. Pass through yet another gate to the road.

Turn right along this country lane with Addlebrough now on your right, and after approximately one mile pass through a gate across the road. After a further quarter of a mile, extensive views of Semerwater and the river Bain are obtained through a field-gate on your left.

Observe carefully a tubular steel field-gate on your right, a further 20 yards along the road at a point where the road begins to descend steeply. Pass through this gate, turn half left and proceed on a well-defined grass track with a stone wall on your left. Ignoring the first field-gate in this wall, continue with the wall on your immediate left until a field-gate in a wall has to be passed through to reach open moorland. From this point a fine view of Askrigg can be obtained on your left.

Straight ahead you will observe another gate through which you should pass. Continue for a further 30 yards, again with the wall on your left, until the track turns left through a field-gate in this wall. The track now descends sharply, swinging round to the right, passing through a further gate and entering a walled lane leading to the road and the farmstead of Cubeck.

Turn right along the road, climbing steadily for the first few hundred yards, and continue for a little over a mile to Thornton Rust. From this road extensive views of Wensleydale can be enjoyed.

Distance : *7 miles.*

SEMERWATER

Starting Point : *Centre of the village of Bainbridge, G.R. 934901.*

Public Transport : *Bainbridge is served by United Automobile Services Routes* 26 (*Hawes - Darlington*) *and* 127 (*Hawes - Ripon*).

LEAVE Bainbridge along a lane between the post office-cum-shop on the left and the chapel on the right. After approximately 30 yards, turn right along another lane towards a field-gate. Bear right and follow a footpath, rising slightly, with a stone wall on your right. Pass through the gap in the stone wall, still climbing steadily, and swing round to the right until a stile is reached. Follow a well-defined footpath gradually veering away from the wall on your right towards a stone wall with a wooden-gated stile. The river Bain lies immediately on your left down a steep slope. The way continues with a stone wall on your right, and then passes the stone barn on the right to a stile in the wall ahead, slightly left of the barn. Go half right to the corner of the field, climbing steadily, to pass through a further stone stile. Aim towards the left of the farm on the hill in front of you until you cross a stile in a stone wall, and then make your way uphill to the farm (Gill Edge). On reaching the cart track, turn right and follow the track past the front of the house through an iron field-gate and on to the metalled road. Turn left and follow the road until the village of Countersett is reached.

Continue through Countersett, and just beyond note the first view of Semerwater. Leave the village by proceeding along the Marsett road for approx. 120 yards until you pass a solitary tree on your right. Cross over some sheep-wire near to the tree, at a point where the stile used to be, and turn left and veer slightly away from the road to go through a stile in the wall ahead. Keeping in the same general direction with the road to your left, pass through the next two stone walls by broken-down gaps (path indistinct). The next stile ahead is difficult to negotiate and lies to the right of an ash tree. Still keeping in the same direction cross the next field with barn on your right and a further stile ahead. A wire fence will now be observed on your left. On reaching the ruins of Thorns House, pass to the right, cross a bridge over a stream and turn half right to an iron-wicket gate to approach Wood End Lodge. Follow the footpath round the back of the house and turn left on to the cart track to join the metalled road, along which you turn right for Marsett.

In Marsett village turn left by the telephone box and follow the cart-track with Bardale Beck on your left. After fording Raydale Beck cross over the footbridge fifty yards further to the left. Turn left, and follow the stone wall on the right for fifty yards to cross it by means of a stone stile. Turn left and follow the wall to a stone barn, beyond which you pass a stone stile on your left under a tree. Then go straight ahead over a narrow field (40 yards) to another stone stile, and then a further stile 100 yards ahead. Go forward, with a dilapidated stone barn on your left, rising slightly past a belt of trees by a stream. Pass through another stile, cross the water-course under the trees, and continue straight ahead through a succession of stone stiles with the village of Stalling Busk on your right.

In due course pass the ruins of an old church on your left to follow a well-defined path through a succession of six stiles, the last of which is adjacent to the left-hand side of a barn and affords entry to a field to reach the shores of Semerwater. Follow the shore until you gain the road through an iron field gate near a bridge.

Turn left along the road, and then right through a stone-stile in the parapet of Semerwater Bridge immediately before crossing the river Bain. Make for the far right-hand corner of the first field and pass through a gap in the wall. The path is straight ahead towards a barn and through a field-gate to the left of the barn. Go straight ahead with the wall on your left to yet another barn and through a gap to the right of this. Turn left and, passing the barn on your left, follow the stone wall for some 120 yards until you reach a gap in the wall. Pass through this gap and continue in the same direction with the wall now on your right towards a clearly visible stile, followed by another barn on your right with a gate and stile to the left of it. Passing through this stile, cross over a small rough pasture and pass through a stile in a stone wall ahead. Then follow a succession of stiles over the top of the hill in front of you (Bracken Hill) until you reach the corner of two stone walls

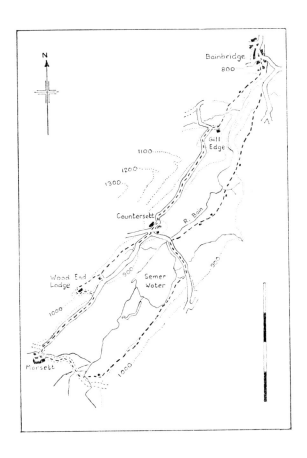

N

Bainbridge
800

Gill
Edge

1100

1200

1300

Countersett

R. Bain

Wood End
Lodge

900

900

Semer
Water

1000

Marsett

1000

in which you will find a gated stile. From this point excellent views are obtained of Wensleydale and the river Bain to your left. Keep straight ahead on a fairly well-defined track, keeping to the right of a sheepfold, to descend into Bainbridge with a wall on your right and the river Bain on your left. On joining the road turn left to reach the village in a few hundred yards.

Distance : 8 *miles.*

HAWES AND DODD FELL

Starting Point : *Centre of Hawes village, G.R.* 874898.

Public Transport : *Hawes is served by United Automobile Services Routes* 26 (*Hawes - Darlington*) *and* 127 (*Hawes - Ripon*).

LEAVE Hawes by passing through the archway opposite the Midland Bank and adjacent to the church. Follow the footpath parallel to Duerley Beck until the Gayle road is reached. Go half left across this road, pass through a stile on to another paved path, and continue along this until another lane is reached. Turn right on to this lane, and then right again at the first T-junction and left at the second. Take the second turning on the right, Gaudy Lane. Follow this track for nearly half-a-mile, until one field from the farm (Gaudy House) and then pass through a gate. You are following the Pennine Way, and your route is by the wall first on the right and then on the left along a well-trodden path in approximately a south-westerly direction.

In due course a green lane is joined, and you bear left along the shoulder of Dodd Fell with the Snaizeholme Valley down on the right. Soon after passing the head of the valley, a junction of three lanes is reached at Kidhow Gate.

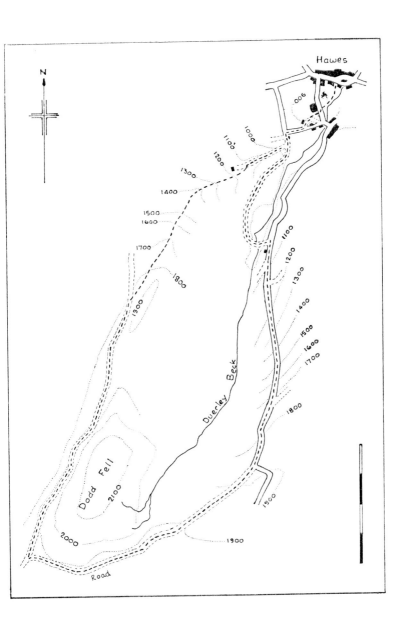

In front the ground falls away into Upper Langstrothdale. Turn left along the narrow metalled road, and follow it for two-and-a-half miles until the motor road from Hawes to Buckden is reached. Follow the road towards Hawes, by carrying straight on at the junction, and descend with the road into Sleddale.

As you reach civilisation, turn off the road to the left just after passing the second stone building on the left, and go along the winding cart-road to cross Duerley Beck by a ford (there is a footbridge a few yards upstream if required). Follow the green lane up the hill side, and in one mile you will reach the end of Gaudy Lane, from where your route back into Hawes is the same as on the outward journey.

Distance : **11** *miles.*

COTTERDALE

Starting Point : *Centre of Hawes village, G.R.* 874898.

Public Transport : *Hawes is served by United Automobile Services Routes* 26 (*Hawes - Darlington*) *and* 127 (*Hawes-Ripon*).

LEAVE Hawes by walking along the Sedbergh road (A684) as far as the hamlet of Appersett, and turn off at the second stile on the left after crossing the bridge over Widdale Beck. Cross the field diagonally; the route is now over a stile near the corner and then, after a second stile, half left uphill.   Crossing the next stile in the corner, and then yet another stile, it goes half left through a gap and continues down towards the river. The footpath is now parallel with the river, but nearly one hundred yards from it, and after four hundred yards it crosses a stile in the wall on the right and then goes down and over a small ditch.   The way is now across the field towards the building ahead from where there is a good view of the dale with Birk Rigg, a large farmstead, on the hill.   Continue to the farm track and turn right to cross the river to return to the main road.

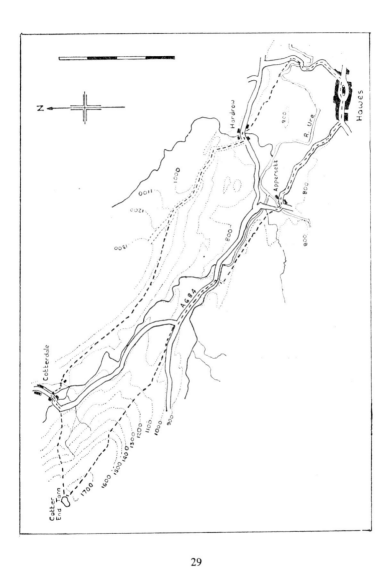

Turn left on the main road, and continue for half-a-mile to the junction with the road to Cotterdale, which can be followed to that village by those who want a shorter walk. Continue along the main road for a little further, and then set off across the open moor to climb Cotter End. It is a fairly steep climb, and the easiest ascent is by keeping to the wall in the centre of the ridge, passing an old lime-kiln near the top from where a glance back gives a magnificent view of Wensleydale. Continue over the brow of the hill, and follow the wall on your left for a short distance before striking off in a north-westerly direction along the boundary fence to Cotter End Tarn, with another good view, this time of Garsdale and the Moorcock Inn, on your left. On leaving Cotter End Tarn, walk due east and very soon look down into Cotterdale village, to which you descend steeply (the route up to Cotter End and down to Cotterdale village is not a definitive right of way).

On reaching the centre of the village the way is to the right (looking up the valley) across a footbridge, and then along a well-defined footpath, following the valley round at about eleven hundred feet above sea level through a succession of stiles. As Hawes comes into view, it climbs a little up the hillside and goes through two field gates to join the green lane which is the Pennine Way. Descend by the Pennine Way into Hardraw, with its famous waterfall which can be seen on application at the local hostelry.

To return to Hawes cross the stile on the right, shortly after crossing the bridge in Hardraw, and then bear round to the left to follow the old paved route, which is still the Pennine Way, across the golf course back to Hawes.

Distance : 10 *miles.*

Swaledale

JOCKEY CAP HILL

Starting Point : Gilling West Bridge, G.R. 183054.

*Public Transport : Gilling West is served by United Auto-
mobile Services Route* 29 (*Darlington - Manfield - Richmond*).

FROM Gilling West Bridge take the twin gates on the
north side of the bridge and follow the line of stiles and
wicket gates upstream to Hartforth, where you turn left
along the narrow road and cross the picturesque stone
bridge. Turn right into the fields and cross the pasture to a
prominent white gate at the north end of the wooded bank.
Go over the plank bridge to the sawmill from where you
continue by the stream side, crossing the narrow road curi-
ously named Comfort Lane. When the streams cut off to
the north, continue westwards along a high green bank to a
double stile. Then go on to a broken stone stile and gate
under the tall trees in the north-west corner of the next pasture. Turn into the field over the gate and then look out for
a stone stile in the hedge on your left; proceed almost due
west to Ravensworth village and castle.

Turn up the road towards Kirby Hill and leave it for a
field road at the first bend. As you approach the large farm,
a stone stile and gate on the left gives access to a field-path
up the hill to Kirby church.

From Kirby take a narrow opening on the south-west
corner of the green and go by a stiled path to Sturdy House
—which comes into view as you climb out of the dip beyond the village. The route is almost due south. Keep this
farm on your right-hand and take the road uphill to the
south. The first lane on your left takes you to Green
Lane Farm. A bridle road across the pastures continues

towards Jockey Cap Hill, and you reach the angle of a wall just above a spreading tree in an old quarry. Turn down the wall side to your right and continue along this half-metalled road to Beacon Cottages on the Richmond — Marske road.

Turn east and beyond the first large farm on your left take the path alongside the gallops. When you leave the gallops turn left down the road to a gate on your right leading alongside to the golf-course. You pass below the golf house and keep on the rough between the fairways to a path running down between the cropped fields at the east end of the golf course. The path enters Aske Park and you cross a rough pasture in a north-easterly direction to the gates of the mansion gardens. A road skirts the east side of the gardens; beyond the "Poultry Centre" take a path through a belt of trees to the main road back to Gilling.

Distance : 8 *miles.*

GRINTON CIRCULAR

Starting Point : *Centre of Grinton village, G.R.* 046984.

Public Transport : *The United Automobile Services Route* 30 (*Richmond - Reeth - Upper Swaledale*) *passes the starting point.*

FROM THE CENTRE of the village take the Aysgarth and Leyburn road which ascends the valley of Grinton Gill away from the river Swale. At the fork about 600 yards away from the centre of the village, take the right-hand (Askrigg) road and follow this until it bends away to the left. At this point a well-defined track will be seen straight ahead, and this is your route.

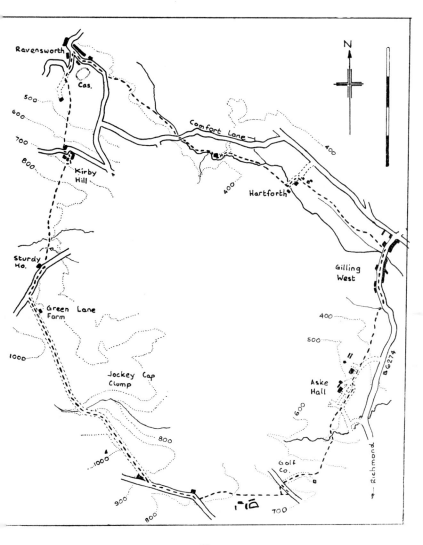

To begin with, the path keeps relatively level and soon crosses Grovebeck Gill, which lower down becomes Grinton Gill. Once the stream is crossed the path begins to ascend Harkerside Fell, keeping the crest of the ridge initially on the right, but after a few hundred yards following it until the plateau is reached on the top of Harker Hill. This is the highest point of the walk, and it is worth pausing to admire the view which includes the lower parts of Arkengarthdale and the sylvan reaches of Swaledale below Grinton. The group of trees, the Jockey Cap near Richmond, is a landmark on the near horizon, and in the far distance the faint grey outline of the Cleveland and Hambleton Hills can be seen.

From this point turn right to begin the descent into Swaledale, and very soon you will be on a distinct path plunging down the hillside. On your left is the view up Upper Swaledale to Great Shunner Fell, the highest point in this area. When you reach the road along the south side of the dale, on an unenclosed stretch, turn left and proceed up the dale. In about half-a-mile the road will begin to descend with a stone wall on the right hand side. Shortly after the road again becomes totally unenclosed—and, as it reaches the valley bottom, turn right along a well-defined footpath. Cross the scrub and pass through a gate in the wall to reach the riverside route back to Grinton.

Initially, your way is along an elevated terrace high above the river, but soon you descend to the river's edge and continue through a copse which lines the river bank. The village of Healaugh can be seen up on the other bank. The path ultimately emerges from the wooded stretch into a large field, which should be crossed to the farthest corner. From here the path is partly enclosed as it keeps immediately below the bluff. As the bluffs recede, it begins to ascend the side of a river-cliff to become a totally enclosed lane which continues to join the metalled road half-a-mile outside Grinton village. The route is then straight on into the centre of the village.

Distance : 6 miles.

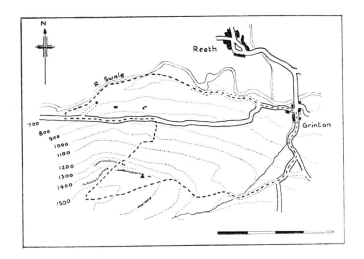

ARKENGARTHDALE

Starting Point : Junction of Reeth - Barnard Castle and Reeth - Tan Hill - Brough roads in the middle of Arkengarthdale, G.R. 998034.

DESCEND TO the Arkle Beck along the Barnard Castle road, and cross a stile on the left just before the bridge over the beck.   Follow the footpath round to the right to cross the footbridge and walk upstream by a succession of stiles in the walls for one-and-a-quarter miles to the hamlet of Whaw.

Continue along the narrow metalled lane for a further half-mile to Faggergill Bridge, where the road inclines sharply to the right.   Leave the road here and go through the gateway on the left and along the farm road to Low Faggergill Farm. Keep along the farm road to the right of the farmhouse and then, on reaching the second gate, look across the moor to the right and see High Faggergill in the distance. There is only a faint cart track across the rough pasture in that direction, but the terrain is easy-going and High Faggergill will soon be reached.

Now go round the back of the farmhouse on to the rough farm road which is routed south at an elevation of 1,300 feet above sea level. After one mile the road begins to drop towards the valley and it is then that further views of Arkengarthdale are revealed. On reaching the narrow lane turn left and in 400 yards you will come to a farmhouse on the right. An alternative return route is to continue from this farmhouse to the Barnard Castle road, and then turn right so as to get back to the start.

Those who wish to return to the start by field-paths should go through the hand-gate at the end of the garden wall, walk diagonally down the field and round past the front of Greenbank Cottage, and then down to the Arkle Beck. Turn left for a few yards, cross the beck by the footbridge and continue downstream for 400 yards. After crossing a shallow gill, climb steadily out of the valley, pass a small farmhouse and keep along the path to a group of houses known as C. B. Terrace, near the starting point, thus completing the walk.

Distance : *5 miles.*

HURST CIRCULAR

Starting Point : *At the south-east corner of the village of Fremington, where the Reeth - Richmond road is joined by a secondary road from Marrick, Marske, Washfold and Hurst, G.R.* 046989.

Public Transport : *United Automobile Services Route* 30 *(Richmond - Reeth - Upper Swaledale) passes the starting point.*

LEAVE THE starting point by walking along the secondary road, signposted to Marske and Marrick, for a very short distance until the first turning on the left is reached. Take

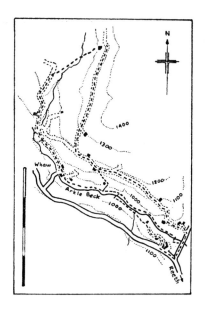

this secondary road, and the left fork a short distance up the hill, and then the next turning right as you pass through the village of Fremington. Turn right at the T-junction, and take the right fork shortly afterwards to join the drove-road up Fremington Edge. As the unmetalled road ascends, the view up Arkengarthdale unfolds itself on the left. In due course you pass through a gate on the top of the edge, and the path makes a gradual descent to the hamlet of Hurst. This is very much former lead-mining country, littered with spoil heaps and the occasional derelict chimney which serve as memorials to the long-departed industry.

The hamlet of Hurst is reached at a T-junction where you turn left, to pass in front of a few cottages on the right and then through a gate back on to the moor. Do not turn right shortly after passing through this gate, even though this might appear to be the main track, but follow the other track straight on. This track is quite distinct as it winds its way through more spoil heaps to the watershed. Immediately after crossing the watershed the route is not quite so plain, but can easily be found by keeping alongside a partly ruined wall to above the valley of Stel Gill. The route then descends the side of the valley and after crossing a very small tributary gill reaches Storthwaite Hall in Arkengarthdale.

The route back to Fremington follows the left bank of Arkle Beck, reached by turning left by Storthwaite Hall. Ignore the footbridge on the right, and keep straight on. Passing a deserted cottage, the footpath ascends somewhat and after some little distance passes through a gate on to the uncultivated moorland. Keep the intake-boundary wall close at hand on your right. After passing another cottage, a walled track will be reached on your right. Follow this down to the next farm, pass through the stile on your left, and follow the footpath through a few fields down the riverside. The route then passes through a gate and into some riverside woodland. It is now quite broad, and after some little distance begins to ascend slightly through the woodland and out into some fields. Once through a succession of fields the track becomes enclosed, and shortly afterwards the fork is reached at the top of Fremington village. The remainder of the walk follows the same route as on the outward journey.

Distance : 7 miles.

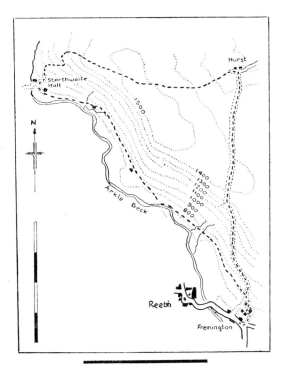

REETH CIRCULAR

Starting Point: *The centre of the village of Reeth, G.R.* 038992.

Public Transport: *Reeth is served by United Automobile Services Route* 30 *from Richmond.*

LEAVE REETH by the Gunnerside and Muker road (B6270) and upon reaching the school turn right up the right-hand side of it to pass through a narrow stile into a field. Cross the field diagonally to another stile, and you will shortly join a lane. Turn left into the lane, which winds its way along the hillside eventually to emerge on to the open pasture on Reeth Low Moor. All cultivated land is left below, and the way is along the open heather moor. Below on the left is Swaledale, with Harkside Moor on the opposite side. Do not ascend the moor on your right, but maintain approximately the same altitude, keeping the stone wall marking the uppermost limit of the intake visible on the left. In due course, the low spur of Feetham Pasture separates you from Swaledale itself, and the valley below is that of Barney Beck. In front of you the road from Feetham over the moor to Arkengarthdale becomes visible, and your way is to follow the contours until the road is reached where it crosses the beck, immediately before the final ascent to cross the watershed between the two dales.

Turn right on joining this road and ascend to the top of the hill, where a broad track goes off through a gate on the right down towards Arkengarthdale. Follow this track with Arkengarthdale apparent below on the left hand, in front, the distinct feature of Fremington Edge. In a little over a mile the main road down Arkengarthdale from Tan Hill to Reeth is reached. The way here is to the right, and for those people in a hurry to return to Reeth, a quick two mile road walk.

For those who wish for a more interesting walk, which is only slightly longer, there is an alternative close to the valley bottom. After walking along the road for about half-a-mile, a broad farm lane is reached on the left. Follow this lane down to the farm buildings, and turn right to pass them. Go through the right hand of two gates opposite and ascend a small hill, keeping a small group of pine trees on the left. Pass through the gate beyond, and the way is now distinct, keeping to the right of the wall at the top of the river cliffs. After passing through a succession of fields a farm track is reached. Bear right along this track and, after passing through a gate, take the footpath in front where the main track bends to the right near a barn. The path carries on through a series of narrow stiles; take care to keep the two barns on the right. Shortly after the second barn, a grey detached house becomes visible in front, and the footpath joins the Tan Hill road in the corner of a field to the right of this house. Turn left and descend to the centre of Reeth.

Distance : **7** *miles.* **40**

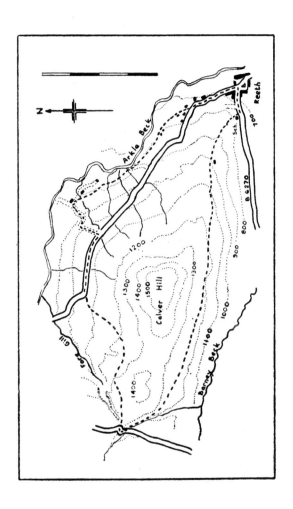

IVELET MOOR

Starting Point : *The centre of Gunnerside village, G.R. 951982.*

Public Transport: Gunnerside is served by United Automobile Services Route 30 from Richmond.

TAKE THE Ivelet road out of Gunnerside; it can be distinguished as the road which follows the left (north) bank of the river upstream from the centre of the village.

Follow this road for about a thousand yards until a cottage with five chimney stacks, Dyke Heads, is reached on the left hand side. Immediately beyond this turn right along a rough track, which ascends the shoulder of the hill and bears left to enter Gunnerside Gill, one of the leading centres of the former lead-mining industry, the main level being known as the Sir Francis Level. Continue along this track until you pass through an iron gate, pass over a small waterfall, and ascend to a green shooting box. Take particular care to follow the left fork behind the shooting box, and to note a line of shooting butts on your left. The path eventually turns left to pass through the heaps of Stony Mine Waste. Very soon, to the left in the distance, can be seen the twin tarns of Moss Dam. Shortly after this another green shooters' hut will be passed before the path descends, with the stream on your left and views ahead of the uppermost reaches of Swaledale, to the mine buildings of Swinnergill.

Cross the beck by the small stone bridge and make for the gate on the skyline, and on to the ruins of the former Crackpot Hall. After passing the hall descend to the wall, and in one hundred yards—before reaching a barn—take the left-hand cart track to descend to another gate and a second small footbridge. After crossing the footbridge, follow the well-defined cart track down the bottom of the dale along

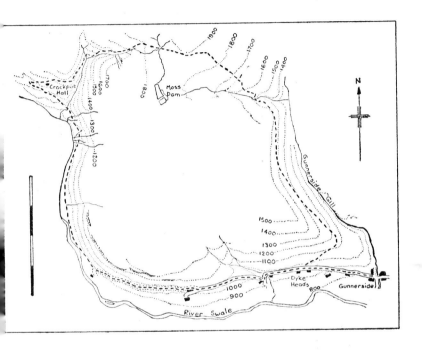

the riverside towards Muker village. Do not cross the river Swale, but keep on the left bank, passing above but not over a white footbridge. In due course this path soon becomes a road, and ultimately returns to Gunnerside, passing Gunnerside Lodge and Dyke Head en route.

Distance: 9½ *miles.*

Teesdale

BOWES CIRCULAR

Starting Point : *Cross-roads at the eastern end of Bowes village, G.R.* 996135.

START BY WALKING along the village street, which is the A66 Brough via Stainmore road, and immediately beyond the Central Garage turn right and then gently left and right through a graveyard of crashed cars to cross the former railway line. Keep to the wall on your left, cross a stile in the corner and then go across the next field and by the wall on your left to Clint Lane. Turn left with a good view across Sleightholme Moor to Tan Hill. Follow this lane, for one-and-a-half miles, ultimately passing West Stoney Keld Farm on your left to go through a gate in the far corner and emerge on to the open moor. Keep the wall surrounding the farm-intake on your left, until a sharp turn in the wall is reached, whereupon you should leave the wall and carry on in a south-westerly direction until a long stone wall is reached. Keep this on your left until you reach the A66 at Pasture End.

At this point the Pennine Way crosses the A66 and a stepping stile on the south side of the road marks the continuation both of your walk and the Pennine Way down to God's Bridge, an arch of limestone spanning the river Greta. Immediately after crossing this natural phenomenon, there is a right-of-way over a dilapidated fence on your left by a ruined lime kiln. Cross this fence and walk up the field to the farm buildings of West Mellwaters. Turn left, go across the field to a ladder stile to take you over the wall, and then forward to a field-gate and by the wall on your left to East Mellwaters.

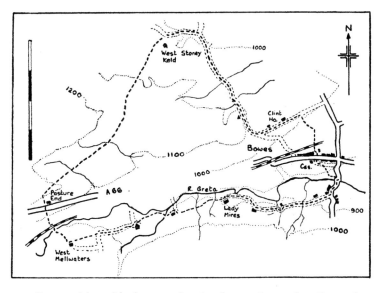

On reaching this farm, take the footpath passing through the left-hand of two adjoining gates and continue diagonally left towards the river Greta, passing through a field-gate a few yards from the river. Follow the river downstream to its confluence with Sleightholme Beck, which should be crossed by stepping stones. At the time of writing the Ramblers' Association is endeavouring to have a footbridge constructed at this point, due to it being on the Bowes diversion of the Pennine Way. Your way is by the front and then the side of the next farm, West Charity Pasture, to turn left on to a good cart road which after passing three farms will take you into the village of Gilmonby. Turn left to follow the metalled road back into Bowes village at the cross-roads at the start of the walk.

Bowes Castle, at the west end of the village and now in the care of the Department of the Environment, is worth a visit. It is a former peel-tower built from the ruins of the

Roman settlement, Lavatrae, as a defence against maraud-
ing Scots.

Distance : 7 *miles.*

BARNARD CASTLE CIRCULAR

Starting Point : *Outside the Butter Market in Barnard Castle,*
G.R. 050163.

Public Transport : *Barnard Castle is well served with buses*
operated by the United Automobile Services, with direct links
with Bishop Auckland and Darlington.

THE WALK starts by going through St. Mary's church-
yard, keeping the church on your right. At the school buildings, turn right between some posts into a lane. Follow this
until open ground is reached, then turn left along a well-
defined track which follows the river Tees, passing through
a wicket gate and between the farm buildings.   Continue
along the track by the river until a stile is reached beside a
gate, immediately beyond which turn right, thereby continu-
ing close to the river. On reaching the wood, cross a stile on
your left and follow the well-defined path to Abbey Bridge.

On reaching the road, cross directly over to a gap in the
wall opposite and, keeping on the same side of the river,
proceed along a well-defined path through the woods until a
wicket-gate is reached. The way is now ahead with a stone
wall on the right and through another wicket-gate. Soon the
ground falls away to the river. At this point, make your way
towards the trees which line the river bank on slightly higher
ground. Now follow the line of the trees, keeping to the left
of a stone wall, until reaching the meeting of the waters
where the river Greta joins the Tees on the opposite bank.

The route now climbs fairly sharply half-left up the field
and underneath the over-head transmission lines. Almost at
the top, and before reaching a field-gate in the corner, a stile
is visible in a stone wall at the topmost fringe of some more
trees. After crossing this stile, continue in the same general

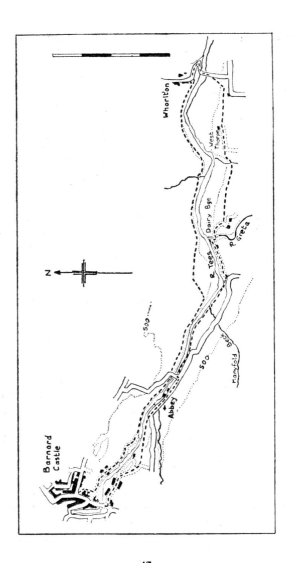

N ←

Barnard
Castle

Whorlton

West
Thorpe

R. Tees

Dairy Bge

R. Greta

Abbey

Mangold Bck

500

500

47

direction, passing through a succession of stiles and gates until you reach Sledwick Gill. Cross the stile in the wall ahead of you (about twelve yards from the right-hand corner of the field), and ford the beck at the head of a picturesque waterfall.

Climb out of the gill up some steps opposite, following the track along the top until you reach a wire fence. Keep this fence on your left and continue along the top of the wood until you cross a stile, from where the fence will be on your right until Whorlton bridge. Between the gill and this point the path is very overgrown. Continue for some 300 yards, and then swing left to the high ground above the trees on your right and walk along the top of the hill until you pass through a field-gate. Continue in the same direction until you see the village of Whorlton, whereupon go through a wooden gate to follow a path between the village and the river until you reach the road. In another ten yards turn down some steps on your right to cross Whorlton suspension bridge.

On the south bank of the river follow the road for about thirty yards and cross a stone stile in a wall on your right. Turn left and go diagonally up the field towards the wood and the house, making for an iron gate in the wall ahead directly beneath some transmission lines. The route now is straight ahead across the cart-track with a wall on your left. After passing through another field-gate with a building on your right, you continue in the same direction with the wall on your right and go through a further field-gate and stile. Bear left round the end of a wooded gill to a gate in the corner, and continue straight ahead with the hedge on your left and the ground sloping away to the river on your right. Pass through a white field-gate and observe Mortham Tower ahead of you.

The route is slightly right to follow the direction of the transmission lines until you reach Dairy Bridge. After crossing over the bridge, turn right with the river Greta on your right for some twenty or thirty yards to the Meeting of the Waters.

Continue along the cart track, and about five yards before reaching the main road you will observe a broken-down gate on your right leading into a wood. This appears to be overgrown, but a path takes you through this wood and emerges on the banks of the river by a fence. Keep this on your right and continue up river. Cross a steep-sided valley (Manyfold Beck) and continue with the fence on your right to enter the wooded riverside path known as Paradise Walk. On approaching Abbey Bridge, the path bears left to climb steeply and join the road.

Keeping on the same side of the river, continue along the road with the river on your right. After passing Egglestone Abbey and the ancient Bow Bridge, cross a stone stile on your right at a point where the road takes a sharp left-hand bend. Keep straight ahead along the footpath, with the fence and the river on your right, to pass through two more stiles and across the top of the caravan park. Passing through an iron wicket gate, continue in the same direction to cross a stile on to a road. Turn right through a caravan park and, where the road swings sharp right, your way is sharp left to cross a stile to the left of a house. Continue ahead past the houses until you observe the metal bridge over the river Tees. Cross this and continue up the hill into Barnard Castle.

Distance: 9 miles.

BARNARD CASTLE — COTHERSTONE

Starting Point: Bottom of Galgate, Barnard Castle, G.R. 049166.

Public Transport: Barnard Castle is well served with buses operated by the United Automobile Services, with direct links with Bishop Auckland and Darlington.

START ALONG the track which passes the right-hand side of the chapel, and descend diagonally down to reach the riverbanks just near to the waterworks bridge. Do not cross over the bridge, but turn right to walk up the left bank of the river to cross Flatts Beck by a rustic bridge. Take the right-hand fork a little further along to ascend the banks of the river to a gated bridle-road affording good views of the surrounding countryside. Follow this until West Holme House is reached shortly after East Holme House has been passed on the right and the shallow gill has been crossed. Keeping to the left of the farm-buildings of West Holme, follow the cart-track through a couple of gates and then turn half-right across the third field. The stile on the far side will lead you to a narrow but well-worn path which descends to a stone slab footbridge. Continue up to the right of a hand-gate in a wall on the far side of the gill, and proceed straight ahead alongside a large field climbing gently over the brow of a hill with the wooded banks close to the left. In due course, after passing through the next stile, the path descends to the banks of the Tees just opposite its confluence with the river Balder. Cross a foot-bridge over the Tees, and then over another one across the Balder into Cotherstone vilage.

Turn left in the village towards Barnard Castle. Near the top of the village, where the main road swings sharp right, turn sharp left round Featherstone House. Two right turns will bring you to the back of the house, and your route is through a gate leading into a field where there are two stone buildings, the farther one belonging to the Society of Friends, and standing in the Quaker Burial Ground. Keep this on the right. Beyond it veer to the right to a slab bridge over a narrow gill, and then turn left, keeping fairly close to the gill and crossing a couple of stiles close together to reach a long narrow field with a wall on the right. At the end of this field, your way is through a gap on the left of a stile and round the back of Cooper's Farm.

Keep close to the wood-side, pass through a couple of gates and turn left between an old barn and the edge of a wood. Adjacent to a log cabin, a high stile with a hinged top-bar leads you on to a track down a broad gill. At the foot of the gill, cross over a stile and stone-slab bridge into Towler Hill Wood and, at the top of the wood, pass through

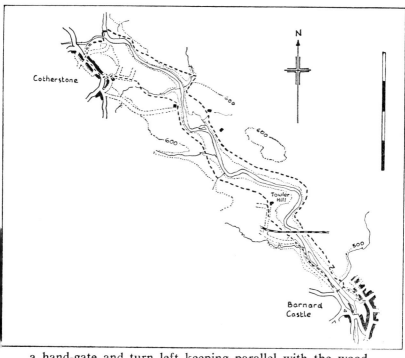

a hand-gate and turn left keeping parallel with the wood-side. There are gates, but little sign of a path. However, the pasture on the west-side of Towler Hill Farm is entered by a distinctive white gate, and you should make for a gap on the far side of the farm. Keep the field boundary on your right, and make your way in a wide arc around the head of the shallow gill to reach a stile up by the woods. Cross the stile, and the track of the former railway, and then descend to the riverside path which brings you back to the water-works bridge. This should be crossed to bring you back on to the outward route, near to the start of the walk.

Distance : **7** *miles.*

BALDERSDALE

Starting Point : *Centre of the village of Cotherstone, G.R.* 012197.

Public Transport : *Cotherstone is served by United Automobile Services Route* 76 (*Darlington - Barnard Castle - Middleton*).

FROM THE centre of the village walk in a northerly direction along the main road towards Middleton-in-Teesdale. Immediately after crossing Balder bridge, your route is over the stile and down the stone steps on the left. Cross the first field diagonally, and then up the bank along a defined path. Go through the field-gate, and follow the fence with the river Balder on your left. The footpath is ahead with the river below, passing through several fields before the old railway-track is reached. Stepping stiles are provided for the crossing of this track from which a good view is obtained of Goldsborough Scar across the valley.

The way is now forward and through a gate, then turning left to follow the cart-road to West End Farm, passing through the farmyard and by the back of the farmhouse. Bear gently to the right, go through the field-gate and make for the distant stile, beyond which the path goes half-right to another stile near a stunted tree. Follow a wire fence to cross a stile and a beck, then forward past a hay-shed from where you will obtain your first glimpse of the spillway from the Hury Reservoir. Veer to the left to go by the end of some bushes down into the gill to cross the stream by the footbridge. Emerging on the opposite side, keep to the wall on your right but on approaching the farmhouse turn sharp right round some buildings. Pass through a gap on the right to cross a stile in the wall on your left, following the footpath to the cross-dale road just to the north of the house which was formerly the Strathmore Arms Inn.

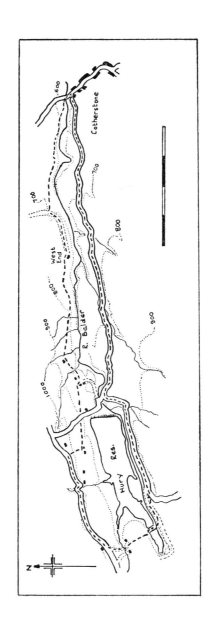

Cross the stile on the opposite side of the road to obtain excellent views of Hury Reservoir. The footpath goes across the stile by the front of the first building reached, passes by the back of the next building, and then continues stile-by-stile in a northerly direction to reach the road along the northern side of the dale. Turn left along the road, and follow it across Howgill Bridge until you turn left again opposite the little chapel on the right to go along the farm road to East Newhouses Farm. Walk round the side and back of this farm, then over a stile in the corner and down the fields to cross the dam between Blackton and Hury Reservoirs. On reaching the metalled road, turn left and return to Cotherstone.

Distance : **9** *miles.*

MIDDLETON CIRCULAR

Starting Point : *Middleton Bridge, where the B6277 (Middleton - Cotherstone - Barnard Castle) crosses the river Tees just south of Middleton, G.R. 947253.*

Public Transport : *Middleton-in-Teesdale is served by United Automobile Services Route* 76 *(Darlington - Barnard Castle - Middleton).*

START BY following the cart-road upstream on the right bank from the bridge. The route is sign-posted "Pennine Way"; it is well-stiled and well defined, and due to the ever-increasing traffic on the Way has become easy to follow. After two miles, however, a careful watch must be kept to see the Holwick Beck as it enters the Tees at the foot of the bank. Here the path drops suddenly, crosses the beck by footbridge and for the remainder of the way keeps close to the river bank. The next footbridge over the Tees is Scorberry, linking Newbiggin with Holwick, and this is followed by Winch Bridge close to Bow Lee.

Then comes Holwick Head Bridge from which the extension to High Force can be made. The Tees must be crossed at this point. Climb on to the road, turning right for a few

In Teesdale country. A view of the river Tees at Barnard Castle (drawn by S. Warburton).

yards, then left along the road towards Ettersgill. The metalled road bends to the left but the route of this walk is to the right to a little group of houses known as Dirt Pit, a corruption of "Durpit," meaning a place where the deer were herded in the days when this area was a great forest. Keeping on in between the row of cottages and farmhouses, the bridle road climbs out of the hollow. Along this elevated road there are some extensive views including the rounded form of Noon Hill above High Force, and still further away is a glimpse of Mickle Fell. Across the valley are Holwick Scar and the fells beyond. After passing through numerous fields, Bow Lee is reached.

Walk the length of this hamlet to cross Bow Lee bridge, and turn left along the track through the disused quarry. Follow the Bow Lee Beck for approximately 500 yards to see Gibson's Cave, a recess in the rock over which there is a waterfall about twenty feet in height. Just above the waterfall is Summer Hill Farm which is on the route of the walk. From the beck climb steeply towards the farm buildings, and then follow the farm road to the lane descending into Newbiggin.

Walk to the end of the village, climb steeply before rounding the bend in the road and then cross the stile on the right where a "Footpath" sign has been erected. Go half-left to a ladder stile and walk by the wall for a few yards before going left to a stile across the field. Now take a route half left across the next field to a stile leading into Ravelin Gill. Walk a few yards into the gill, then keep to the right along a green path, but on reaching a deep depression in the gill turn right to go through a bridle-gate into the open fields. Follow the hedge on the right, going through a second bridle-gate and half left to a large stile in a stone wall just below Bell Farm. Now cross the field towards the farm to reach the exit on to the lane. The last one-and-a-half miles takes you along this quiet lane descending all the while past Middle Side and Lane Head back to Middleton-in-Teesdale.

Distance : **10** *miles.*

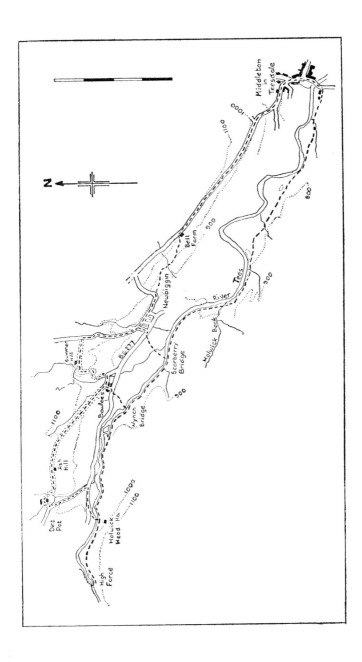

HIGH FORCE

Starting Point : *End of Holwick village,* **G.R. 904271.**

START AT the head of Holwick village, where the sur-faced road makes an acute turn to the right. Follow the track which goes straight ahead at this point into the Nature Reserve. A mile-and-a-half from the start a signpost directs the walker along the official right-of-way, a faint green track which bears right off the more prominent track.

Cross the Blea Beck to see on the left White Force, a slender waterfall which descends into a limestone fissure below. Ascend the green track to the top of Cronkley Fell, following the cairns which mark the path at frequent inter-vals. From the summit, Mickle Fell can be seen on the left and, in front, Cross Fell, the highest point on the Pennines, and its attendant peaks of Great and Little Dun Fell and also the new Cow Green Reservoir.

Descend to the banks of the river Tees, and turn right to follow the river downstream along the foot of Cronkley Scar. In two miles, Cronkley Bridge is reached. Bear right along the farm-road uphill to Cronkley Farm, keeping the buildings on your left and following the defined path to the bottom of the field. Go to the left and then right and climb through the gap in the crags and between the juniper bushes. Through the gap the path is to the left round two sides of a wire fence to a stile in the wall. Over this stile veer to the left along a defined path through more junipers and then drop to the riverside.

Cross three tributaries of the Tees by three footbridges whereupon the route back to Holwick is a well defined path along the banks of the river Tees itself past High Force, Holwick Head Bridge and the Wynch suspension bridge across the river just beyond Low Force. Immediately past this point, the path leaves the river and crosses the fields to Holwick with Holwick Mansion, the Earl of Strathmore's shooting lodge, on the right.

Distance : **12** *miles.*

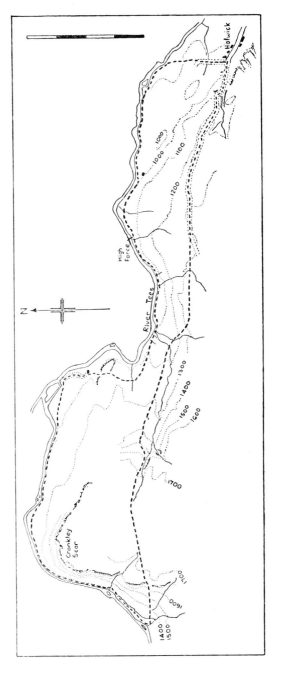

CAULDRON SNOUT

Starting Point: *Adjacent to the Langdon Beck Hotel on the Middleton-in-Teesdale - Alston road, G.R. 854312.*

FROM OUTSIDE the hotel, walk along the main road for a short distance towards Middleton-in-Teesdale, and then turn right along Peghorn Lane to the junction of Harwood Beck and Langdon Beck. Follow the Harwood Beck upstream, cross the cart-bridge and turn right along the road to the first cattle grid. Just before the grid, turn off to the left along the rough cart-road which winds its way over the fell to Widdybank Farm just over a mile away.

On reaching the farmstead, walk down the pasture to the river Tees, at the same time facing the great cliffs of Cronkley Scar dropping steeply from Cronkley Fell to the river below. Begin to walk upstream, the path soon becoming rough and stony as the high bank closes in on the right leaving only a narrow path by the river across large boulders and scree. It is a scramble for a few hundred yards, and then after a stretch of easy progress there is more scrambling over boulders by the river's edge. Although some stretches on this section of the walk are boggy or rocky, it should not present any difficulty to anyone who is reasonably shod. Falcon Clints, a long range of great basaltic cliffs, are ultimately reached, and from here the scenery gradually becomes wilder and more impressive, the river taking a sweep to the north opposite its confluence with Maize Beck. Shortly, you will be confronted with Cauldron Snout, one of England's finest waterfalls, crashing through a rocky gorge to the riverbed 200 feet below. Ascend the side of the waterfall to the bridge carrying the road across the river Tees to the isolated farmhouse at Birkdale. Ahead of you lies the great dam of the Cow Green Reservoir.

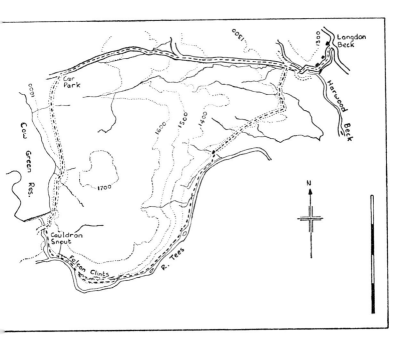

To complete the walk, follow the road past the right-hand end of the dam to reach Peghorn Lane at Cow Green, a disused lead mine, whereupon you should turn right to return to the cars two-and-a-half miles further on at Langdon Beck. Although this road is metalled, it is unfenced, so you can walk on the moor at the roadside.

Distance : **8** *miles.*

HAMSTERLEY FOREST

Starting Point : *The Lido in Hamsterley Forest, one mile to the north-west of the village of Hamsterley, G.R. 093313.*

TAKE THE ROAD westward towards the Grove, and in a quarter of a mile turn left along the forest track which soon crosses Bedburn Beck. Immediately beyond the bridge, a footpath (not too easy to follow in parts) goes to the right alongside the river, and then works its way up through the trees to rejoin the main track a quarter of a mile further on. This path is part of a forest trail, about which a descriptive leaflet is obtainable. Continue along the track until it meets a metalled road, then turn right for a few hundred yards and branch right again along another downhill track. This brings you over another bridge across the Bedburn Beck back on to the Grove road. Turn left here and follow the road to the Grove itself — a large country house owned by the Forestry Commission but usually let to a tenant.

From the Grove turn right, cross Euden Beck by a footbridge near to a ford and follow the track uphill to a clearer area above the forest workers' smallholdings. In about 1,000 yards one comes to a spot where five tracks meet, G.R. 068309. Take the rightmost track downhill to a footbridge across the Ayhope Beck, and go straight up the other side on a less well-defined track between the two walls. Cross over a forest road and continue up to a gate at the forest boundary — go through the gate and turn right. This track, sometimes a little boggy, may be followed until a corner of the forest is reached. The forest is entered again, and a track continues eastward to join the metalled approach road to the Lido, 300 yards to the north.

Those wishing to take the longer walk should follow the instructions in the first paragraph until the Grove is reached. From here, follow the footpath along the side of Euden Beck to cross the beck and pass a cottage. In about half-

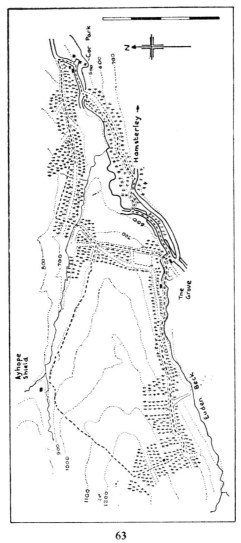

a-mile take a branch track which goes off to the right. Continue along this track for another mile, ignoring a right turn, to reach a junction where a track comes in towards you on the left, and a ride with a footpath goes off to the right, G.R. 041297. This path to the right ascends to Black Hill at the forest boundary, from where the way, now ill-defined, goes north-east for about a mile to reach Ayhope Shield, G.R. 049316.

It is not necessary to cross the South Grain Beck to Ayhope Shield itself, since the way now turns right near to the beck. Keep parallel with the water until you hit a nasty bog about a hundred yards from the forest boundary. This bog can be avoided by keeping to the right, but it may be crossed with care if conditions are not very bad. Enter the forest by the gate through the wall, and follow the track to the five lane ends, G.R. 068309. Take the path on the second left, and return to the start by the route described in the latter half of the second paragraph.

Distance : *5 miles (shorter route).*

10 *miles (longer route; it is unwise to follow this in poor visibility, since in such conditions it is confusing, particularly between Black Hill and Ayhope Shield).*